© 2024 by FAISAL JAMIL. All rights reserved.

Title: "The Harmony of Team: A Comprehensive Guide to Effective Team Management"

This book, along with its contents encompassing text, illustrations, images, diagrams, and other creative elements, is the exclusive property of FAISAL JAMIL and is safeguarded by copyright law.

FAISAL JAMIL asserts full ownership and retains all rights to this book. No part of this publication may be reproduced, distributed, or transmitted in any form or by any means, such as photocopying, recording, or electronic methods, without prior written consent from the copyright holder. Brief quotations in critical reviews and certain noncommercial uses permitted by copyright law are exceptions.

This copyright notice applies to all editions, formats, and translations of the book, whether in print, digital, or any other medium or technology existing now or developed in the future. Unauthorized use or infringement may result in legal action and pursuit of remedies under applicable copyright laws.

While efforts have been made to ensure accuracy and reliability, FAISAL JAMIL does not guarantee the completeness or suitability of the information. Readers are responsible for evaluating and using the content judiciously.

FAISAL JAMIL reserves the right to make changes, updates, or corrections to the book without prior notice. Inclusion of third-party materials or references does not imply endorsement or affiliation unless used under fair use principles or with proper permissions and attributions.

For permissions, inquiries, or requests regarding the book's use, please contact FAISAL JAMIL through official channels listed on their Amazon author page or provided email address.

This comprehensive copyright notice serves to protect FAISAL JAMIL'S intellectual property rights, maintain content control, and inform users about associated restrictions and permissions.

Warm regards,

FAISAL JAMIL

For your feedback and reviews:

https://www.amazon.com/author/faisal.jamil

Email: faisaljamilauthor@gmail.com

About the author

Certainly! Faisal Jamil is a multifaceted individual with a diverse set of skills and experiences. With a strong foundation in computer knowledge since childhood, he has developed a deep understanding of technology that informs his work as a content writer. Faisal also possesses digital skills, which further enhance his abilities in various digital platforms and technologies.

Beyond his professional endeavors, Faisal Jamil has also excelled in the martial arts, particularly Shotokan Karate, where he achieved the prestigious rank of first Dan black belt. This achievement speaks to his dedication, discipline, and commitment to personal growth and mastery.

In his professional life, Faisal Jamil has carved out a successful career in sales management within the Fast Moving Consumer Goods (FMCG) sector. His roles in various FMCG companies have honed his skills in strategic planning, team leadership, and business development. Faisal's ability to drive sales and achieve targets has been instrumental in his career progression, showcasing his talent for identifying opportunities and delivering results.

Faisal Jamil is also deeply interested in business investment strategies, planning, and execution. His understanding of these areas has been key to his success in the business world, allowing him to make informed decisions and implement effective strategies. His ability to navigate the complexities of investment planning and execution has set him apart as a strategic thinker and a valuable asset in any business endeavor.

Overall, Faisal Jamil is a dynamic individual who combines his passion for technology, martial arts, sales management, digital skills, and business investment strategies to achieve success in diverse fields. His journey is a testament to his versatility, resilience, and continuous pursuit of excellence.

Yours Sincerely

FAISAL JAMIL

For your feedback and reviews:

https://www.amazon.com/author/faisal.jamil

Email: faisaljamilauthor@gmail.com

THE HARMONY OF TEAM

A COMPREHENSIVE GUIDE TO EFFECTIVE

TEAM MANAGEMENT

Table of Content

Preface 7

Chapter 1: Understanding Team Dynamics 10

Chapter 2: Building a Strong Team 20

Chapter 3: Leadership in Team Management 31

Chapter 4: Managing Remote Teams 42

Chapter 5: Team Performance Evaluation 51

Chapter 6: Developing Team Skills 62

Chapter 7: Leading Change in Teams 71

Chapter 8: Case Studies in Team Management 81

Chapter 9: The Future of Team Management 87

Chapter 10: Conclusion 92

Preface:

Welcome to "The Harmony of Team: A Comprehensive Guide to Effective Team Management." This book is designed to be a practical and comprehensive resource for anyone involved in managing teams. Whether you are a seasoned team leader or a new manager, this book is intended to provide you with valuable insights and strategies for building and leading high-performing teams.

In today's fast-paced and dynamic work environment, effective team management is more important than ever. Teams are often responsible for driving innovation, solving complex problems, and achieving organizational goals. However, managing teams effectively can be challenging, especially in a world where teams are increasingly diverse, geographically dispersed, and reliant on technology.

This book is divided into several chapters, each focusing on a different aspect of team management. We start by exploring the fundamentals of team dynamics, including the importance of understanding the different types of teams and the stages of team development. We then delve into practical strategies for building a strong team, establishing clear goals and objectives, creating a positive team culture, and fostering effective communication and collaboration.

Throughout the book, we also address common challenges in team management, such as handling conflict, motivating team members, and managing remote teams. We provide practical tips and techniques for overcoming these challenges and building a cohesive and high-performing team.

One of the key themes of this book is the importance of leadership in team management. Effective leadership is essential for guiding and motivating team members, fostering a positive team culture, and driving team performance. We provide insights into the qualities of a good team leader, different leadership styles, and strategies for delegating responsibilities and motivating team members.

We also explore the role of change management in team management. In today's rapidly changing world, teams are often required to adapt to new challenges and opportunities. We provide strategies for leading change effectively, communicating change, involving team members in the change process, and overcoming resistance to change.

Finally, we look towards the future of team management, exploring trends such as remote and hybrid work, digital transformation, and the importance of diversity and inclusion. We provide strategies for adapting to these changing work environments and ensuring long-term success.

Throughout the book, we draw on real-life examples, case studies, and practical exercises to help illustrate key concepts and provide readers with actionable insights. Our goal is to provide you with a practical and comprehensive guide to effective team management that you can apply in your own work.

We hope that you find this book to be a valuable resource in your journey to becoming a more effective team manager. Whether you are leading a small project team or a large organization, the principles and strategies outlined in this book can help you build and lead teams that achieve success.

Thank you for choosing "The Harmony of Team: A Comprehensive Guide to Effective Team Management." We wish you success in your team management endeavors.

Chapter 1: Understanding Team Dynamics

A: Introduction to Team Management

Team management is a multifaceted process that involves various aspects of leadership and organization to ensure that a group of individuals can work together efficiently and effectively towards a common goal. It encompasses a range of activities, including planning, organizing, leading, and controlling, all aimed at maximizing the team's performance and achieving the desired outcomes.

1: Planning:

Team management begins with setting clear goals and objectives for the team. This involves defining the scope of work, establishing timelines, and determining the resources needed to achieve the goals. Planning also involves identifying potential risks and developing strategies to mitigate them.

2: Organizing:

Once the goals and objectives are established, the team manager must organize the team in a way that best utilizes the skills and talents of its members. This may involve assigning roles and responsibilities, creating work schedules, and establishing communication channels.

3: Leading:

Effective leadership is crucial in team management. A good leader inspires and motivates team members, provides guidance and direction, and resolves conflicts. Leadership also involves setting a positive example for the team and creating a supportive and inclusive team culture.

4: Controlling:

Controlling involves monitoring the team's progress towards its goals and making adjustments as needed. This may involve tracking key performance indicators, conducting regular performance reviews, and addressing any issues or challenges that arise.

Overall, effective team management requires a combination of planning, organization, leadership, and control to ensure that the team works together cohesively and achieves its objectives. By focusing on these key aspects, team managers can create a positive and productive team environment that fosters collaboration, innovation, and success.

B: Importance of Team Dynamics

Team dynamics play a crucial role in the success of a team. They refer to the way team members interact with each other, the relationships they form, and the processes they use to achieve their goals. Understanding team dynamics is essential because they can significantly impact team performance and productivity.

1: Impact on Team Performance:

Positive team dynamics can lead to improved performance. When team members work well together, they can leverage each other's strengths, collaborate effectively, and achieve better results. On the other hand, negative team dynamics can lead to conflicts, misunderstandings, and a lack of cohesion, which can hinder performance.

2: Enhanced Creativity and Innovation:

Positive team dynamics can foster creativity and innovation. When team members feel comfortable sharing their ideas and collaborating with others, they are more likely to come up with innovative solutions to problems. In contrast, negative team dynamics can stifle creativity and discourage team members from sharing their ideas.

3: Effective Problem-Solving:

Positive team dynamics can also improve problem-solving abilities. When team members trust and respect each other, they can work together more effectively to identify and address issues. Conversely, negative team dynamics can lead to ineffective problem-solving and a lack of progress.

4: Conflict Resolution:

Team dynamics can influence how conflicts are handled within a team. Positive team dynamics can lead to constructive conflict resolution, where team members are able to address issues openly and find mutually beneficial solutions. In contrast, negative team dynamics can result in destructive conflicts that harm relationships and hinder progress.

5: Morale and Engagement:

Team dynamics can also impact morale and engagement. When team members feel valued, supported, and respected, they are more likely to be engaged in their work and motivated to perform well. Negative team dynamics, on the other hand, can lead to low morale and disengagement.

In conclusion, understanding and managing team dynamics are essential for creating a positive and productive team environment. By fostering positive team dynamics, teams can enhance their performance, creativity, and problem-solving abilities, ultimately leading to greater success.

C: Types of Teams

There are several types of teams, each serving a different purpose within an organization:

1: Functional Teams:

These teams are organized based on the functions or departments within an organization, such as marketing, finance, or operations. Functional teams typically consist of members with similar skills and expertise who work together to achieve the goals of their department.

2: Cross-Functional Teams:

Cross-functional teams consist of members from different functional areas within an organization who come together to work on a specific project or task. These teams bring together diverse perspectives and expertise to solve complex problems and achieve common goals.

3: Virtual Teams:

Virtual teams are teams whose members are geographically dispersed and rely on technology to communicate and collaborate. Virtual teams are becoming increasingly common in today's globalized world, as they allow organizations to tap into a larger talent pool and operate across different time zones.

4: Project Teams:

Project teams are formed to work on specific projects with a defined start and end date. These teams are temporary and are disbanded once the project is completed. Project teams typically consist of members with relevant skills and expertise needed to complete the project successfully.

5: Self-Managed Teams:

Self-managed teams are responsible for managing their own work and making decisions collectively. These teams are empowered to set their own goals, allocate tasks, and solve problems independently. Self-managed teams are often highly motivated and can be more efficient and effective than traditional hierarchical teams.

Each type of team has its own unique characteristics and challenges. By understanding the different types of teams and their purposes, organizations can better structure their teams to achieve their goals and objectives.

D: Stages of Team Development

Tuckman's stages of team development provide a framework for understanding the evolution of a team over time. Here's a detailed look at each stage:

1: Forming:

a: Characteristics: In this initial stage, team members are introduced to each other and are often polite and friendly. They may be anxious about the future and unsure about their roles.

b: Activities: Team members focus on getting to know each other, building relationships, and understanding the goals of the team.

c: Leadership: Leadership is crucial in providing direction and clarity to team members during this stage.

2: Storming:

a: Characteristics: Conflicts and disagreements may arise as team members start to establish their roles and compete for influence within the team.

b: Activities: Team members may challenge each other's ideas and opinions, leading to debates and arguments. It's important for the team to work through these conflicts constructively.

c: Leadership: Leadership is key in managing conflicts, facilitating discussions, and helping the team find common ground.

3: Norming:

a: Characteristics: In this stage, the team begins to establish norms and rules for working together. Trust and cohesion start to develop among team members.

b: Activities: Team members start to understand and respect each other's strengths and weaknesses. They collaborate more effectively and begin to align their efforts towards achieving the team's goals.

c: Leadership: Leadership focuses on reinforcing positive behavior, encouraging collaboration, and building a sense of unity within the team.

4: Performing:

a: Characteristics: The team is now fully functional and achieves high levels of productivity. Team members work together seamlessly and autonomously, leveraging each other's strengths to achieve common goals.

b: Activities: The focus is on delivering results and continuously improving performance. Team members are motivated and committed to the team's success.

c: Leadership: Leadership is more about providing support and guidance, rather than direct supervision. Leaders empower team members to make decisions and take ownership of their work.

5: Adjourning:

a: Characteristics: This final stage occurs when the team is disbanded after completing its task or project. There may be a sense of sadness or loss as team members say goodbye to each other.

b: Activities: Team members reflect on their achievements and celebrate their successes. They may also discuss lessons learned and how they can apply them in future projects.

c: Leadership: Leadership focuses on helping team members transition out of the team, acknowledging their contributions, and maintaining positive relationships for future collaboration.

By understanding these stages of team development, leaders can better support their teams through each stage and help them achieve high levels of performance and success.

E: Common Challenges in Team Dynamics Some common challenges in team dynamics include:

1: Communication Issues:

Poor communication is one of the most common challenges in team dynamics. It can lead to misunderstandings, conflicts, and a lack of clarity. Effective communication is essential for ensuring that team members are on the same page and working towards the same goals.

2: Conflict Resolution:

Conflict is inevitable in any team, but how it is managed can impact team dynamics. Effective conflict resolution involves addressing issues promptly, listening to all parties involved, and finding a mutually acceptable solution. Failure to resolve conflicts can lead to resentment and hinder team performance.

3: Lack of Trust:

Trust is a fundamental component of effective teamwork. Without trust, team members may be reluctant to collaborate, share ideas, or take risks. Building trust takes time and requires open communication, reliability, and consistency in behavior.

4: Leadership Issues:

Leadership plays a crucial role in shaping team dynamics. Poor leadership can result in directionless teams, lack of motivation, and confusion about roles and responsibilities. Effective leaders inspire and motivate team members, provide clear direction, and facilitate communication and collaboration.

5: Diversity and Inclusion:

Managing diverse teams can be challenging due to differences in perspectives, backgrounds, and working styles. It's essential to create an inclusive environment where all team members feel valued and respected. This involves understanding and accommodating different viewpoints, fostering open communication, and addressing any biases or stereotypes.

By recognizing these common challenges in team dynamics, teams and leaders can take proactive steps to address them and create a more positive and productive team environment. This may include improving communication strategies, implementing conflict resolution processes, building trust among team members, developing strong leadership skills, and promoting diversity and inclusion.

Understanding team dynamics is essential for effective team management. By recognizing the different types of teams, stages of team development, and common challenges, team leaders can create a positive and productive team environment.

Chapter 2: Building a Strong Team

A: Recruiting the Right Team Members

Recruiting the right team members is a critical step in building a strong and effective team. Here's a detailed look at the process:

1: Identifying Skills, Experience, and Qualities:

The first step in recruiting the right team members is to clearly define the skills, experience, and qualities needed for the team. This involves understanding the requirements of the role, the goals of the team, and the overall culture of the organization.

2: Sourcing Candidates:

Once the requirements are defined, the next step is to source candidates who meet these criteria. This can be done through various channels, including job boards, social media, professional networks, and employee referrals.

3: Screening Resumes:

The recruitment process typically begins with screening resumes to identify candidates who meet the basic requirements of the role. This helps narrow down the pool of candidates and identify those who are most likely to be a good fit for the team.

4: Conducting Interviews:

The next step is to conduct interviews with the shortlisted candidates. Interviews can be conducted in person, over the phone, or via video conferencing. The purpose of the interview is to assess the candidate's skills, experience, and fit with the team and organization.

5: Assessing Fit:

In addition to assessing skills and experience, it's important to assess the candidate's fit with the team and organization.

This includes evaluating their personality, communication style, work ethic, and cultural fit.

6: Reference Checks:

Before making a final decision, it's important to conduct reference checks to verify the candidate's qualifications and experience. This can help validate the information provided by the candidate and ensure that they are a good fit for the team.

7: Making an Offer:

Once a suitable candidate has been identified, the next step is to make an offer of employment. The offer should include details such as salary, benefits, start date, and any other relevant information.

8: Onboarding:

Once the offer is accepted, the final step is to onboard the new team member. This involves introducing them to the team, providing them with the necessary training and resources, and setting them up for success in their new role.

By following these steps, organizations can recruit the right team members who are aligned with the team's goals and values, ultimately leading to a stronger and more effective team.

B: Establishing Team Goals and Objectives

Setting clear goals and objectives is a critical step in effective team management. Here's a detailed look at how to establish team goals and objectives:

1: Specific:

Goals should be clear and specific, outlining exactly what needs to be achieved. Vague goals can lead to confusion and lack of direction. For example, instead of setting a goal to "increase sales," a specific goal would be to "increase sales by 10% in the next quarter."

2: Measurable:

Goals should be measurable so that progress can be tracked and evaluated. This helps team members stay motivated and provides a clear indication of whether the goal has been achieved. For example, a measurable goal would be to "generate 100 new leads per month."

3: Achievable:

Goals should be challenging but attainable. Setting goals that are too difficult can demotivate team members, while setting goals that are too easy may not push them to perform their best. It's important to consider the team's resources and capabilities when setting goals.

4: Relevant:

Goals should be relevant to the overall objectives of the team and the organization. They should align with the team's purpose and contribute to the larger goals of the organization. Setting goals that are not relevant can lead to wasted effort and resources.

5: Time-bound:

Goals should have a specific timeframe for completion. This helps create a sense of urgency and keeps the team focused on achieving the goal within a set period. For example, a time-bound goal would be to "launch the new product by the end of the year."

To establish team goals and objectives, it's important to involve team members in the goal-setting process. This helps create buy-in and commitment from team members, increasing the likelihood of success. Additionally, goals should be reviewed regularly to track progress and make any necessary adjustments. By setting clear, specific, measurable, achievable, relevant, and time-bound goals, teams can stay focused, motivated, and on track to achieve their objectives.

C: Creating a Positive Team Culture

A positive team culture is essential for promoting collaboration, trust, and mutual respect among team members. It sets the tone for how team members interact with each other and can significantly impact team performance and satisfaction. Here are some key elements of creating a positive team culture:

1: Open Communication:

Encourage open and honest communication among team members. Create opportunities for team members to share their ideas, concerns, and feedback. This helps build trust and ensures that everyone is on the same page.

2: Constructive Feedback:

Provide constructive feedback to team members to help them improve their performance. Feedback should be specific, timely, and focused on behaviors or actions, rather than personal characteristics. Encourage team members to give each other feedback as well, fostering a culture of continuous improvement.

3: Supportive Environment:

Create a supportive environment where team members feel comfortable taking risks and making mistakes. Encourage a growth mindset, where failures are seen as learning opportunities. Support team members in their professional development and provide resources to help them succeed.

4: Shared Values and Goals:

Establish shared values and goals that align with the team's purpose and objectives. This helps create a sense of unity and purpose among team members, driving them towards a common goal.

5: Recognition and Appreciation:

Recognize and appreciate the contributions of team members. Celebrate achievements and milestones, both big and small. This helps boost morale and motivation within the team.

6: Diversity and Inclusion:

Foster a culture of diversity and inclusion where all team members feel valued and respected. Encourage different perspectives and ideas, as they can lead to more innovative solutions.

7: Lead by Example:

As a leader, it's important to lead by example and embody the values and behaviors you want to see in your team. Be transparent, fair, and empathetic in your interactions with team members.

Creating a positive team culture takes time and effort, but the benefits are well worth it. A positive team culture can lead to higher levels of engagement, productivity, and satisfaction among team members, ultimately leading to better outcomes for the team and the organization.

D: Effective Communication within the Team

Effective communication within a team is crucial for fostering collaboration, building trust, and achieving common goals. Here's how to promote effective communication within your team:

1: Open and Honest Communication:

Encourage team members to communicate openly and honestly with each other. Create a safe space where team members feel comfortable sharing their thoughts, ideas, and concerns.

2: Clear and Concise Messaging:

Ensure that communication is clear, concise, and to the point. Avoid using jargon or overly technical language that may be difficult for others to understand.

3: Active Listening:

Encourage active listening among team members. This means listening attentively to others, asking clarifying questions, and showing empathy and understanding.

4: Use of Multiple Communication Channels:

Utilize a variety of communication channels, such as email, instant messaging, and video conferencing, to ensure that information is communicated effectively to all team members.

5: Regular Updates and Check-ins:

Schedule regular updates and check-ins to keep team members informed of progress, changes, and upcoming tasks. This helps ensure that everyone is on the same page and working towards the same goals.

6: Feedback and Recognition:

Provide regular feedback to team members on their performance. Recognize and appreciate their contributions, which can help boost morale and motivation.

7: Conflict Resolution:

Address conflicts and disagreements promptly and constructively. Encourage team members to resolve conflicts through open dialogue and mutual understanding.

8: Encourage Collaboration:

Promote collaboration among team members by encouraging them to work together on tasks and projects.

This can help build a sense of camaraderie and shared purpose.

By promoting effective communication within your team, you can create a positive and productive work environment where team members feel valued, respected, and motivated to achieve their goals.

E: Encouraging Collaboration and Creativity

Collaboration and creativity are essential for a strong and successful team. Here's how you can encourage these aspects within your team:

1: Create a Collaborative Environment:

Foster a culture of collaboration by encouraging team members to work together towards common goals. Provide opportunities for team members to collaborate on projects and share their ideas and expertise.

2: Promote Open Communication:

Encourage open and transparent communication among team members. Create channels for sharing ideas, feedback, and information, and ensure that everyone has a voice.

3: Value Diverse Perspectives:

Recognize the value of diverse perspectives and encourage team members to consider different viewpoints. This can lead to more innovative solutions and better decision-making.

4: Provide Opportunities for Brainstorming:

Organize brainstorming sessions to generate new ideas and solutions. Encourage team members to think creatively and explore unconventional ideas.

5: Reward Creativity:

Recognize and reward creativity and innovation within the team. This can help motivate team members to think outside the box and come up with new and innovative solutions.

6: Encourage Risk-Taking:

Encourage team members to take calculated risks and try new approaches. Create a safe environment where failure is seen as a learning opportunity rather than a setback.

7: Provide Resources and Support:

Provide the necessary resources and support for team members to collaborate effectively and pursue creative ideas. This may include access to training, tools, and technologies.

8: Lead by Example:

As a leader, lead by example and demonstrate your commitment to collaboration and creativity. Encourage your team members to do the same.

By encouraging collaboration and creativity within your team, you can foster a positive and innovative work environment where team members are motivated to work together towards common goals. This can lead to improved performance, increased job satisfaction, and ultimately, greater success for the team and the organization.

By focusing on recruiting the right team members, establishing clear goals, creating a positive team culture, fostering effective communication, and encouraging collaboration and creativity, team leaders can build a strong and successful team that is capable of achieving its goals and objectives.

Chapter 3: Leadership in Team Management

A: Qualities of a Good Team Leader

Good team leaders possess a variety of qualities that enable them to effectively lead their teams. These qualities include:

1: Clear Communication:

Good leaders communicate clearly and effectively, ensuring that team members understand their roles, responsibilities, and goals. They are able to articulate their vision for the team and provide clear direction.

2: Empathy:

Good leaders are empathetic and understand the needs and concerns of their team members. They are able to relate to others and build strong relationships based on trust and respect. They take the time to listen to their team members and address their concerns.

3: Decisiveness:

Good leaders are decisive and able to make tough decisions when necessary. They are able to weigh the pros and cons of different options and choose the best course of action for the team. They are not afraid to take risks and are willing to stand by their decisions.

4: Problem-solving Skills:

Good leaders are adept at solving problems and overcoming challenges. They are able to think creatively and find innovative solutions to complex problems. They are able to anticipate potential problems and take proactive steps to address them.

5: Adaptability:

Good leaders are adaptable and able to respond effectively to changing circumstances. They are able to adjust their approach as needed to achieve the best results for the team. They are open to new ideas and willing to change course if necessary.

6: Positive Attitude:

Good leaders maintain a positive attitude, even in the face of adversity. They inspire and motivate their team members to do their best and remain optimistic about the team's ability to succeed.

7: Lead by Example:

Good leaders lead by example and set a positive example for their team members to follow. They demonstrate the values and behaviors they expect from others and are willing to roll up their sleeves and pitch in when needed.

8: Resilience:

Good leaders are resilient and able to bounce back from setbacks. They remain calm and composed under pressure and are able to persevere in the face of challenges.

By possessing these qualities, good team leaders are able to inspire and motivate their team members, foster collaboration and creativity, and achieve success for the team and the organization.

B: Different Leadership Styles

Leadership styles can vary greatly depending on the situation and the needs of the team. Here are some common leadership styles:

1: Authoritarian Leadership:

In this style, the leader makes decisions without input from team members and expects them to follow instructions. This style can be effective in situations where quick decisions need to be made or where there is a need for strong direction.

2: Democratic Leadership:

In this style, the leader involves team members in the decision-making process and encourages their input and feedback. This style can help build trust and collaboration within the team, as team members feel valued and respected.

3: Laissez-faire Leadership:

In this style, the leader takes a hands-off approach and allows team members to make their own decisions. This style can be effective when team members are highly skilled and motivated, as it allows them the freedom to innovate and take ownership of their work.

4: Transformational Leadership:

In this style, the leader inspires and motivates team members to achieve their full potential and to work towards common goals. This style focuses on building strong relationships and empowering team members to achieve greatness.

5: Transactional Leadership:

In this style, the leader focuses on the exchange of rewards and punishments to motivate team members. This style can be effective in achieving short-term goals but may not foster long-term commitment from team members.

6: Servant Leadership:

In this style, the leader prioritizes the needs of the team members above their own. The leader serves as a mentor and coach, empowering team members to grow and succeed.

7: Charismatic Leadership:

In this style, the leader uses their charisma and charm to inspire and motivate team members. This style can be effective in rallying team members around a shared vision or goal.

8: Coaching Leadership:

In this style, the leader focuses on developing the skills and abilities of team members through coaching and mentoring. This style can help build a strong and skilled team over time.

Each leadership style has its own strengths and weaknesses, and effective leaders are able to adapt their style to suit the needs of the situation and the team. By understanding different leadership styles, leaders can become more effective in their roles and better support their teams towards achieving success.

C: Delegating Responsibilities

Delegating responsibilities is a crucial skill for team leaders as it allows them to distribute workload efficiently, develop team members' skills, and focus on strategic tasks. Here's how to effectively delegate responsibilities:

1: Assess Tasks:

Start by assessing the tasks that need to be delegated. Identify tasks that can be easily transferred to team members and match them with the skills and capabilities of individual team members.

2: Choose the Right Person:

Consider the strengths, skills, and workload of each team member when delegating tasks. Assign tasks to individuals who are best suited to complete them successfully.

3: Set Clear Expectations:

Clearly communicate the task's objectives, deadlines, and expected outcomes. Ensure that the team member understands the importance of the task and how it fits into the larger goals of the team.

4: Provide Adequate Resources:

Ensure that the team member has access to the resources, information, and support needed to complete the task successfully. This may include training, tools, or assistance from other team members.

5: Monitor Progress:

Regularly check in with the team member to monitor progress and provide feedback. Offer support and guidance as needed to ensure that the task is completed on time and to the expected standard.

6: Encourage Autonomy:

Empower team members to take ownership of their tasks and make decisions independently. Encourage them to seek help if needed but also trust them to complete the task without micromanaging.

7: Provide Recognition and Feedback:

Acknowledge and appreciate the efforts of team members when they successfully complete delegated tasks. Provide constructive feedback to help them improve their skills and performance.

8: Evaluate and Learn:

After the task is completed, evaluate the outcome and the process. Identify any areas for improvement and use this feedback to inform future delegation decisions.

Effective delegation not only helps distribute workload but also empowers team members, develops their skills, and fosters a sense of ownership and accountability. By mastering the art of delegation, team leaders can improve team performance and achieve better results.

D: Motivating Team Members

Motivating team members is essential for keeping them engaged and productive. Good leaders use a variety of techniques to motivate their teams, including:

1: Setting Clear Goals and Objectives:

Clear goals provide team members with a sense of purpose and direction. When team members understand what is expected of them, they are more motivated to work towards achieving those goals.

2: Providing Feedback:

Regular feedback helps team members understand how they are performing and what they can do to improve. Constructive feedback that is specific, timely, and focused on behaviors can help team members stay motivated and engaged.

3: Recognizing and Rewarding Achievements:

Recognizing and rewarding team members for their accomplishments can boost morale and motivation. This can be done through verbal praise, awards, bonuses, or other incentives that are meaningful to the team members.

4: Encouraging Teamwork:

Encouraging teamwork fosters a sense of camaraderie and collaboration among team members. When team members feel like they are part of a supportive team, they are more motivated to work together towards common goals.

5: Providing Development Opportunities:

Offering opportunities for professional development and growth can motivate team members to perform at their best. This could include training programs, mentorship opportunities, or opportunities for advancement within the organization.

6: Creating a Positive Work Environment:

A positive work environment where team members feel valued, respected, and supported can significantly impact their motivation levels. Leaders can create a positive work environment by promoting work-life balance, encouraging open communication, and fostering a culture of trust and respect.

7: Leading by Example:

Leaders who lead by example and demonstrate a strong work ethic, positive attitude, and commitment to excellence can inspire and motivate their team members to do the same.

8: Tailoring Motivation Strategies:

Recognizing that different team members may be motivated by different things, good leaders tailor their motivation strategies to individual preferences. Some team members may be motivated by monetary rewards, while others may be motivated by opportunities for growth or recognition.

By using these techniques, leaders can effectively motivate their team members and create a positive and productive work environment.

E: Handling Conflict within the Team

Conflict is a natural part of team dynamics, but how it is managed can significantly impact team performance and cohesion. Here are some strategies for handling conflict within the team:

1: Addressing Issues Promptly:

Good leaders address conflicts as soon as they arise, rather than allowing them to escalate. They create a safe space for team members to express their concerns and work towards a resolution.

2: Encouraging Open Communication:

Good leaders foster an environment of open communication, where team members feel comfortable expressing their thoughts and feelings. They encourage active listening and ensure that all voices are heard.

3: Finding Common Ground:

Good leaders help team members find common ground and work towards a mutually acceptable solution. They encourage empathy and understanding among team members, helping them see things from each other's perspectives.

4: Seeking Outside Help if Needed:

In some cases, it may be necessary to seek outside help to resolve conflicts. This could involve bringing in a mediator or facilitator to help facilitate discussions and find a resolution that is acceptable to all parties.

5: Setting Ground Rules:

Good leaders set clear ground rules for how conflicts should be handled within the team. This could include guidelines for respectful communication, active listening, and seeking to understand before being understood.

6: Focusing on Solutions, Not Blame:

Good leaders focus on finding solutions to conflicts rather than assigning blame. They encourage a forward-looking approach, where the focus is on how to move past the conflict and work together effectively.

7: Following Up:

After a conflict has been resolved, good leaders follow up with team members to ensure that the resolution is working and that any lingering issues are addressed. They provide support and guidance to help prevent future conflicts.

By effectively managing conflict within the team, leaders can create a more harmonious and productive work environment, where team members feel valued and motivated to do their best.

By possessing the qualities of a good leader, understanding different leadership styles, delegating responsibilities effectively, motivating team members, and handling conflict within the team, leaders can effectively manage their teams and achieve success.

Chapter 4: Managing Remote Teams

A: Benefits and Challenges of Remote Teams Benefits:

Remote teams, where members work from different locations, offer several benefits and challenges:

Benefits:

1: Flexibility:

Remote work allows team members to have more flexibility in terms of their work hours and location. This can lead to increased job satisfaction and work-life balance.

2: Cost Savings:

Remote work can lead to cost savings for both employees and employers. Employees can save on commuting costs and expenses related to working in an office, while employers can save on overhead expenses.

3: Access to Global Talent:

Remote work allows organizations to access a larger pool of talent from around the world. This can lead to a more diverse and skilled workforce.

4: Improved Work-Life Balance:

Remote work can help employees achieve a better work-life balance by allowing them to work from home or other locations. This can lead to increased productivity and job satisfaction.

Challenges:

1: Communication Barriers:

Remote teams may face challenges in communication, as they rely heavily on digital communication tools. Misunderstandings can occur more easily, and team members may feel isolated.

2: Collaboration Difficulties:

Collaborating on projects remotely can be challenging, as team members may not have the same level of interaction as they would in a physical office. This can lead to delays and inefficiencies in project completion.

3: Team Cohesion:

Building a sense of team cohesion and culture can be more challenging in remote teams. Team members may feel disconnected from each other, leading to a lack of trust and camaraderie.

4: Monitoring and Accountability:

Ensuring that remote team members are productive and accountable can be challenging for managers. It can be difficult to track progress and performance without physical supervision.

Overall, remote teams offer many benefits, but they also present unique challenges that need to be addressed to ensure their success. Effective communication, collaboration tools, and a strong team culture are key to overcoming these challenges and maximizing the benefits of remote work.

B: Tools and Technologies for Remote Team Management

Managing remote teams effectively requires the use of tools and technologies that facilitate communication, collaboration, and productivity. Here are some key tools and technologies for remote team management:

1: Communication Tools:

Communication is key for remote teams. Tools like Slack, Microsoft Teams, and Zoom facilitate real-time messaging, video conferencing, and file sharing, enabling team members to stay connected and collaborate effectively.

2: Project Management Tools:

Project management tools like Asana, Trello, and Jira help remote teams organize tasks, track progress, and manage projects efficiently. These tools enable team members to see what needs to be done, who is responsible, and the deadlines for each task.

3: Time Tracking Tools:

Time tracking tools like Toggl and Harvest help remote teams track the time spent on different tasks and projects. This can help managers monitor productivity, identify bottlenecks, and allocate resources effectively.

4: Collaboration Tools:

Collaboration tools like Google Workspace (formerly G Suite), Microsoft Office 365, and Dropbox Paper enable remote teams to collaborate on documents, spreadsheets, and presentations in real-time. These tools allow team members to edit and comment on files, ensuring that everyone is working on the latest version.

5: Virtual Whiteboards:

Virtual whiteboard tools like Miro and Mural are useful for brainstorming, planning, and visualizing ideas. These tools allow remote teams to collaborate on a virtual canvas, making it easy to capture and organize thoughts and ideas.

6: File Sharing and Storage:

File sharing and storage tools like Google Drive, Dropbox, and OneDrive enable remote teams to share and access files securely from anywhere. These tools ensure that team members have access to the latest documents and can collaborate on them in real-time.

7: Security and Privacy Tools:

Security and privacy are important considerations for remote teams. Tools like VPNs (Virtual Private Networks) and password managers help ensure that remote team members can access company resources securely and protect sensitive information.

By leveraging these tools and technologies, remote teams can overcome the challenges of distance and collaborate effectively, leading to increased productivity and success.

C: Strategies for Effective Communication and Collaboration

Effective communication and collaboration are crucial for the success of remote teams. Here are some strategies to enhance communication and collaboration within remote teams:

1: Set Clear Communication Expectations:

Establish clear guidelines for how and when team members should communicate. This includes defining preferred communication channels (e.g., email, chat, video calls) and response times to ensure timely communication.

2: Use Video Conferencing for Important Meetings:

Video conferencing helps improve communication by allowing team members to see each other's facial expressions and body language, which can enhance understanding and build rapport.

3: Foster a Culture of Open Communication:

Encourage team members to share ideas, ask questions, and provide feedback openly and honestly. Create a safe environment where team members feel comfortable expressing their thoughts and opinions.

4: Schedule Regular Check-ins:

Regular team meetings and one-on-one meetings are essential for staying connected and aligned. These check-ins provide opportunities to discuss progress, address challenges, and ensure everyone is on the same page.

5: Use Collaboration Tools:

Utilize collaboration tools to facilitate teamwork and project management. Tools like shared documents, project management software (e.g., Asana, Trello), and virtual whiteboards (e.g., Miro, Mural) help teams collaborate effectively and stay organized.

6: Establish a Communication Plan:

Develop a communication plan that outlines how information will be shared, who will be responsible for communication tasks, and how feedback will be received and addressed.

7: Encourage Feedback and Input:

Encourage team members to provide feedback and input on team processes and projects. This fosters a sense of ownership and involvement among team members.

8: Clarify Roles and Responsibilities:

Ensure that team members understand their roles and responsibilities within the team. Clear expectations help prevent misunderstandings and improve collaboration.

9: Celebrate Achievements:

Recognize and celebrate team achievements to boost morale and motivation. This can be done through virtual celebrations, shoutouts in team meetings, or rewards for outstanding performance.

10: Provide Training and Support:

Offer training and support to help team members improve their communication and collaboration skills. This can include workshops, resources, and coaching.

By implementing these strategies, remote teams can enhance their communication and collaboration, leading to increased productivity, engagement, and overall team success.

D: Building Trust and Accountability in Remote Teams

Building trust and accountability in remote teams is essential for team success. Here are some strategies to achieve this:

1: Establish Clear Expectations:

Clearly define roles, responsibilities, and goals for each team member. Ensure that everyone understands what is expected of them and how their work contributes to the overall goals of the team.

2: Encourage Transparency:

Encourage team members to be open and transparent about their work progress, challenges, and successes. This helps build trust and ensures that everyone is on the same page.

3: Provide Regular Feedback:

Provide regular feedback to team members to help them improve and grow. Feedback should be specific, constructive, and timely, focusing on both strengths and areas for improvement.

4: Promote Team Bonding:

Organize virtual team-building activities and social events to help team members get to know each other better. This can include virtual coffee breaks, online games, or group chats outside of work-related discussions.

5: Recognize and Reward Achievements:

Recognize and reward team members for their hard work and contributions to the team. This can be done publicly in team meetings or privately through personal messages or emails.

6: Encourage Collaboration:

Encourage collaboration among team members by promoting teamwork and sharing best practices. This helps build a sense of camaraderie and collective ownership of team goals.

7: Lead by Example:

As a leader, lead by example and demonstrate trustworthiness and accountability in your own actions. This sets a positive example for team members to follow.

8: Establish Clear Communication Channels:

Ensure that there are clear communication channels in place for team members to raise concerns, ask questions, and provide feedback. This helps prevent misunderstandings and promotes open communication.

9: Provide Support and Resources:

Provide team members with the support and resources they need to succeed. This can include access to training, tools, and information that will help them perform their jobs effectively.

By implementing these strategies, remote teams can build trust and accountability, leading to improved communication, collaboration, and overall team performance.

Chapter 5: Team Performance Evaluation

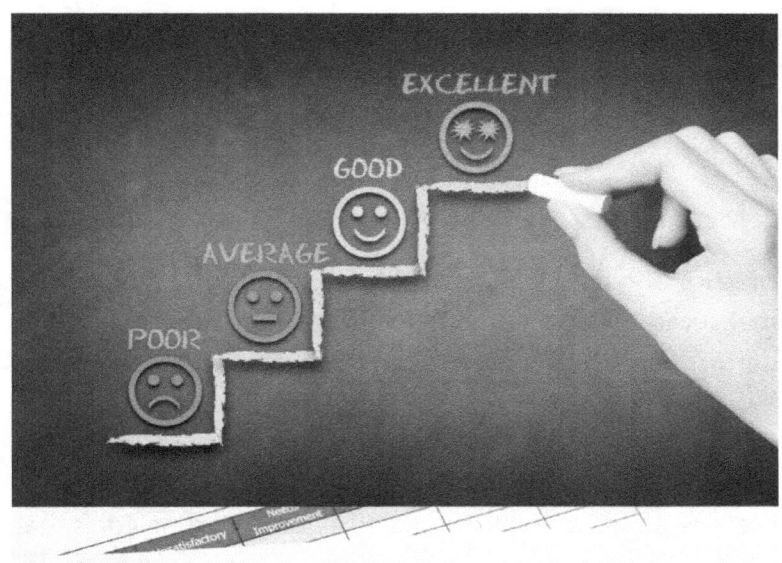

A: Setting Performance Metrics

Setting performance metrics is a crucial aspect of managing a team effectively. These metrics provide a clear framework for evaluating team performance and identifying areas for improvement. Here's how to set performance metrics:

1: Specific:

Metrics should be specific and clearly defined. For example, instead of setting a vague goal like "improve customer satisfaction," a specific metric could be "increase customer satisfaction ratings by 10% within six months."

2: Measurable:

Metrics should be quantifiable so that progress can be measured. Use numbers or percentages to track performance. For example, "reduce customer complaints by 20%."

3: Achievable:

Metrics should be realistic and attainable. Setting goals that are too ambitious can demotivate team members. Consider past performance and resources available when setting goals.

4: Relevant:

Metrics should be relevant to the overall goals of the team and organization. Ensure that the metrics align with the team's objectives and contribute to the organization's success.

5: Time-bound:

Metrics should have a specific time frame for achievement. This helps create a sense of urgency and accountability. For example, "increase sales by 15% by the end of the quarter."

Examples of performance metrics for teams include:

a: Team Productivity:

Measure the team's output or efficiency. This could be the number of tasks completed, projects delivered on time, or revenue generated.

b: Customer Satisfaction:

Measure how satisfied customers are with the team's products or services. This could be done through surveys, feedback forms, or reviews.

c: Project Completion Rates:

Measure the percentage of projects completed on time and within budget. This can help identify areas where the team may need to improve its project management processes.

Setting performance metrics helps teams stay focused and motivated, provides a benchmark for evaluating performance, and enables teams to identify areas for improvement.

B: Conducting Regular Performance Reviews

Conducting regular performance reviews is crucial for assessing team performance, providing feedback, and identifying areas for improvement. Here's how to conduct effective performance reviews for teams:

1: Schedule Regular Reviews:

Set a schedule for performance reviews, such as quarterly or annually, to ensure they are conducted consistently. This allows for regular feedback and keeps performance goals on track.

2: Prepare for the Review:

Before the review, gather relevant information, such as performance metrics, feedback from peers and clients, and examples of the team's work. This will provide a comprehensive view of the team's performance.

3: Create a Positive Environment:

Conduct the review in a private and comfortable setting. Start the review by acknowledging the team's achievements and strengths to set a positive tone.

4: Discuss Performance Metrics:

Review the team's performance against the metrics that were set. Discuss areas where the team has excelled and areas where there is room for improvement. Use specific examples to illustrate your points.

5: Provide Constructive Feedback:

Offer feedback that is specific, constructive, and actionable. Focus on behaviors and outcomes rather than personality traits. Provide suggestions for improvement and offer support to help the team achieve their goals.

6: Encourage Self-Assessment:

Encourage team members to reflect on their own performance and identify areas for improvement. This can help them take ownership of their development and set meaningful goals for the future.

7: Set Clear Goals:

Work with the team to set clear, achievable goals for the future. These goals should be aligned with the team's objectives and should address areas identified for improvement during the review.

8: Follow Up:

Schedule follow-up meetings to track progress on the goals set during the review. Offer support and guidance to help the team achieve their goals.

9: Document the Review:

Keep a record of the performance review, including the discussion points, agreed-upon goals, and any action plans. This documentation can serve as a reference for future reviews and performance evaluations.

By conducting regular performance reviews, teams can assess their performance, identify areas for improvement, and set goals for the future. This process helps teams stay motivated, focused, and aligned with the organization's objectives.

C: Providing Constructive Feedback

Constructive feedback is a powerful tool for improving team performance and fostering professional growth. Here's how to provide constructive feedback effectively:

1: Be Specific:

Provide specific examples of the behavior or actions you are addressing. This helps the team member understand exactly what they did well or what needs improvement.

2: Be Timely:

Provide feedback as soon as possible after the observed behavior or action. This ensures that the feedback is relevant and can be acted upon promptly.

3: Focus on Behavior, Not Personality:

Feedback should focus on specific behaviors or actions, not on the individual's personality or character. This helps keep the feedback constructive and avoids personal attacks.

4: Be Balanced:

Provide a balanced view of the team member's performance, highlighting both strengths and areas for improvement. This helps maintain morale and motivation while also encouraging growth.

5: Be Clear and Direct:

Be clear and direct in your feedback, avoiding vague or ambiguous language. Clearly communicate what you observed and why it is important.

6: Encourage Dialogue:

Encourage the team member to ask questions and seek clarification. This helps ensure that they understand the feedback and are able to act on it effectively.

7: Offer Solutions:

When providing feedback on areas for improvement, offer specific suggestions or solutions. This helps the team member understand how they can improve and gives them a clear path forward.

8: Follow Up:

Follow up on the feedback to see if the team member has made progress. This shows that you are invested in their development and helps reinforce the importance of the feedback.

9: Provide Positive Reinforcement:

Acknowledge and praise the team member for their strengths and achievements. Positive reinforcement can help motivate the team member and build confidence.

By providing constructive feedback, managers can help team members identify areas for improvement, develop their skills, and ultimately improve team performance.

D: Recognizing and Rewarding Team Achievements

Recognizing and rewarding team achievements is essential for boosting morale, motivating team members, and reinforcing positive behavior. Here's how to effectively recognize and reward team achievements:

1: Verbal Praise:

A simple "thank you" or public acknowledgment of the team's achievements can go a long way in boosting morale. Verbal praise should be specific and sincere, highlighting the team's specific contributions and the impact of their efforts.

2: Awards and Certificates:

Recognize team achievements with awards or certificates. These can be presented in a team meeting or ceremony to celebrate the team's success and show appreciation for their hard work.

3: Bonuses or Incentives:

Consider providing bonuses or other incentives to reward team achievements. This can be based on specific performance metrics or milestones achieved by the team.

4: Team Outings or Celebrations:

Organize a team outing or celebration to mark a significant achievement. This could be a team lunch, dinner, or a fun activity to celebrate the team's success and build camaraderie.

5: Professional Development Opportunities:

Offer professional development opportunities as a reward for team achievements. This could include training programs, workshops, or conferences that help team members enhance their skills and knowledge.

6: Flexibility or Time Off:

Provide flexibility or extra time off as a reward for team achievements. This can help team members recharge and maintain a healthy work-life balance.

7: Personalized Rewards:

Consider personalized rewards that cater to the interests and preferences of individual team members. This shows that you value their contributions and are attentive to their needs.

8: Continuous Feedback and Recognition:

Provide regular feedback and recognition for ongoing achievements, not just major milestones. This helps maintain motivation and engagement over time.

9: Transparent Criteria:

Ensure that the criteria for recognition and rewards are transparent and fair. This helps build trust and ensures that team members understand what is expected of them.

By recognizing and rewarding team achievements, managers can foster a positive work environment, motivate team members, and encourage continued success.

E: Strategies for Improving Team Performance

Improving team performance is essential for achieving organizational goals and maintaining a competitive edge. Here are some strategies to enhance team performance:

1: Setting Clear Goals and Objectives:

Clearly define the team's goals and objectives to provide direction and focus. Goals should be specific, measurable, achievable, relevant, and time-bound (SMART).

2: Providing Training and Development Opportunities:

Invest in training and development programs to enhance team members' skills and knowledge. This can improve performance and boost morale.

3: Encouraging Collaboration and Teamwork:

Foster a collaborative environment where team members can work together effectively. Encourage communication, sharing of ideas, and mutual support.

4: Identifying and Addressing Performance Issues:

Monitor team performance regularly and address any issues or challenges promptly. Provide constructive feedback and support to help team members improve.

5: Celebrating Success:

Recognize and celebrate team achievements to boost morale and motivation. This can include verbal praise, rewards, or team celebrations.

6: Promoting Work-Life Balance:

Encourage a healthy work-life balance to prevent burnout and improve productivity. Offer flexible work arrangements and support well-being initiatives.

7: Providing Resources and Support:

Ensure that team members have the resources and support they need to perform their jobs effectively. This includes access to tools, technology, and training.

8: Setting Clear Roles and Responsibilities:

Clarify each team member's role and responsibilities within the team. This helps avoid confusion and ensures that everyone knows what is expected of them.

9: Encouraging Innovation and Creativity:

Foster a culture of innovation and creativity where team members are encouraged to think outside the box and explore new ideas.

10: Monitoring and Evaluating Performance:

Regularly monitor team performance against goals and objectives. Use performance metrics to track progress and identify areas for improvement.

By implementing these strategies, organizations can improve team performance, increase productivity, and achieve better results.

By setting performance metrics, conducting regular performance reviews, providing constructive feedback, recognizing and rewarding team achievements, and implementing strategies for improving team performance, managers can help their teams achieve greater success and productivity.

Chapter 6: Developing Team Skills

A: Training and Development Programs

Training and development programs are crucial for enhancing team skills, knowledge, and capabilities. These programs provide team members with the necessary tools and resources to excel in their roles and contribute effectively to the team. Here's how to develop and implement effective training and development programs:

1: Identify Training Needs:

Conduct a training needs assessment to identify the skills and knowledge gaps within the team. This can be done through surveys, interviews, and performance evaluations.

2: Set Clear Objectives:

Define clear objectives for the training program, outlining what skills or knowledge team members are expected to gain by the end of the program.

3: Choose the Right Training Methods:

Select training methods that are suitable for the team's needs and learning preferences. This could include workshops, seminars, online courses, or on-the-job training.

4: Tailor Training Programs:

Customize training programs to meet the specific needs of the team. Focus on developing skills that are directly relevant to their roles and responsibilities.

5: Provide Ongoing Support:

Offer ongoing support and resources to help team members apply the skills and knowledge they have learned during training. This could include access to mentors, coaching, or additional learning materials.

6: Evaluate Training Effectiveness:

Regularly evaluate the effectiveness of training programs to ensure they are meeting the team's learning objectives. This can be done through surveys, feedback sessions, or performance evaluations.

7: Encourage Continuous Learning:

Foster a culture of continuous learning within the team. Encourage team members to seek out new learning opportunities and stay updated on industry trends and best practices.

8: Measure Training Impact:

Measure the impact of training programs on team performance and effectiveness. This could include tracking key performance indicators (KPIs) related to the skills or knowledge gained through training.

By investing in training and development programs, organizations can improve team performance, enhance employee satisfaction, and stay competitive in today's fast-paced business environment.

B: Building Emotional Intelligence in Team Members

Emotional intelligence (EI) is a key factor in effective teamwork and leadership. It involves understanding and managing emotions, both in oneself and in others. Here are some strategies for building EI in team members:

1: Encourage Self-Awareness:

Help team members develop self-awareness by encouraging reflection on their own emotions, strengths, and weaknesses. This can help them understand how their emotions impact their behavior and interactions with others.

2: Develop Empathy:

Empathy is the ability to understand and share the feelings of others. Encourage team members to practice empathy by listening actively, considering others' perspectives, and showing compassion.

3: Promote Effective Communication:

Effective communication is essential for building EI. Encourage team members to express their emotions and thoughts openly and honestly, while also being respectful of others' feelings.

4: Provide Feedback:

Offer constructive feedback to help team members understand how their emotions and behavior impact others. This can help them develop self-awareness and improve their emotional intelligence.

5: Manage Stress:

Help team members develop strategies for managing stress and emotions in challenging situations. This can include techniques such as deep breathing, mindfulness, and time management.

6: Encourage Collaboration:

Foster a collaborative team environment where team members feel comfortable sharing their emotions and working together to find solutions to problems.

7: Lead by Example:

As a leader, demonstrate emotional intelligence in your own interactions with team members. This can help set a positive example and encourage others to develop their EI.

8: Provide Training:

Offer training programs on emotional intelligence to help team members develop their EI skills. This can include workshops, seminars, or online courses.

By building emotional intelligence in team members, organizations can create a more positive and productive team environment. Team members who are emotionally intelligent are better able to understand and manage their own emotions, communicate effectively with others, and navigate interpersonal relationships more successfully.

C: Encouraging Continuous Learning and Growth

Encouraging continuous learning and growth is essential for keeping team members engaged, motivated, and competitive in today's fast-paced work environment. Here are some strategies for promoting continuous learning and growth within your team:

1: Provide Access to Learning Resources:

Offer access to a variety of learning resources, such as books, articles, online courses, and webinars. Encourage team members to explore topics that interest them and are relevant to their roles.

2: Support Further Education:

Support team members who wish to pursue further education, such as certifications, diplomas, or degrees. This can help them develop new skills and advance their careers.

3: Offer Professional Development Opportunities:

Provide opportunities for team members to attend workshops, seminars, and conferences related to their field. This can help them stay current with industry trends and best practices.

4: Encourage Knowledge Sharing:

Encourage team members to share their knowledge and expertise with others. This can be done through informal discussions, presentations, or workshops within the team.

5: Promote a Growth Mindset:

Foster a culture of continuous learning and growth by promoting a growth mindset. Encourage team members to view challenges as opportunities for learning and development.

6: Set Learning Goals:

Encourage team members to set learning goals for themselves and regularly review their progress. This can help them stay focused and motivated to continue learning.

7: Recognize and Reward Learning Achievements:

Recognize and reward team members who actively engage in continuous learning and demonstrate growth. This can help reinforce the importance of lifelong learning within the team.

8: Lead by Example:

As a leader, demonstrate a commitment to continuous learning and growth. Share your own learning experiences and encourage others to do the same.

By encouraging continuous learning and growth, organizations can create a culture of learning that supports team members in developing their skills, staying current with industry trends, and achieving their career goals.

D: Building Resilience in the Team

Resilience is a crucial trait for teams to navigate challenges, setbacks, and changes effectively. Here are strategies to build resilience within your team:

1: Promote a Positive and Supportive Team Culture:

Foster a positive and supportive team culture where team members feel valued, supported, and encouraged to take risks and learn from failures. This can help build resilience by providing a strong support system.

2: Encourage Open Communication:

Encourage open and honest communication within the team. This can help team members feel more comfortable sharing their thoughts, feelings, and concerns, which can strengthen team bonds and resilience.

3: Provide Resources for Stress Management:

Offer resources and support for stress management, such as mindfulness practices, wellness programs, and access to counseling services. This can help team members cope with stress and build resilience.

4: Set Realistic Goals and Expectations:

Set realistic goals and expectations for the team. This can help prevent burnout and feelings of overwhelm, which can undermine resilience.

5: Encourage Flexibility and Adaptability:

Encourage team members to be flexible and adaptable in the face of change. This can help them navigate uncertainties and challenges more effectively.

6: Celebrate Successes and Learn from Failures:

Celebrate team successes and use failures as learning opportunities. This can help build resilience by fostering a growth mindset and encouraging team members to see setbacks as temporary obstacles.

7: Provide Opportunities for Professional Development:

Offer opportunities for team members to develop new skills and knowledge. This can help build confidence and resilience by expanding their capabilities and increasing their ability to adapt to new challenges.

8: Lead by Example:

As a leader, demonstrate resilience in your own behavior. This can help set a positive example for the team and inspire them to develop their own resilience.

By building resilience in the team, organizations can create a more resilient and high-performing team that can effectively navigate challenges and thrive in today's dynamic work environment.

Chapter 7: Leading Change in Teams

A: Understanding Change Management

Change management is a structured approach to transitioning individuals, teams, and organizations from a current state to a desired future state. It involves defining and instilling new values, attitudes, norms, and behaviors within an organization to ensure that the change is successful.

1: Identifying the Need for Change:

The first step in change management is to identify the need for change. This could be due to internal factors, such as outdated processes or technology, or external factors, such as market trends or competition.

2: Creating a Change Management Plan:

Once the need for change has been identified, a change management plan is created. This plan outlines the goals of the change, the timeline for implementation, and the resources required.

3: Communicating the Change:

Communication is key during the change management process. Leaders need to communicate the reasons for the change, the benefits it will bring, and how it will impact the team. This helps to get buy-in from team members and reduces resistance to the change.

4: Managing the Transition Process:

During the transition process, it is important to manage the change effectively. This may involve providing training to team members, updating processes and procedures, and providing support to help team members adapt to the change.

5: Monitoring and Evaluating the Change:

Once the change has been implemented, it is important to monitor and evaluate its impact. This helps to ensure that the change is achieving its goals and identify any areas that need further improvement.

6: Sustaining the Change:

Sustaining the change involves embedding the new behaviors, processes, and attitudes into the organization's culture. This may involve reinforcing the change through rewards and recognition, and ensuring that it is integrated into all aspects of the organization.

Overall, understanding change management is important for leaders as it helps them to effectively navigate change and ensure that it is implemented successfully. By following a structured approach to change management, leaders can minimize disruptions to the team and ensure that the change is embraced by all stakeholders.

B: Communicating Change Effectively

Effective communication is essential when leading change in teams. It helps team members understand the reasons for the change, the benefits it will bring, and their role in the change process. Here are some strategies for communicating change effectively:

1: Be Clear and Transparent:

Clearly communicate the reasons for the change, the benefits it will bring, and the impact it will have on the team. Avoid using jargon or technical language that may confuse team members.

2: Use Multiple Communication Channels:

Use a variety of communication channels to reach team members, such as team meetings, emails, newsletters, and intranet updates. This ensures that everyone receives the information they need.

3: Provide Regular Updates:

Provide regular updates on the progress of the change, including any milestones or achievements. This helps to keep team members informed and engaged in the change process.

4: Listen to Feedback:

Be open to feedback from team members and address any concerns or questions they may have. This shows that their input is valued and can help to alleviate any fears or resistance to the change.

5: Lead by Example:

Demonstrate your commitment to the change by leading by example. This can help to inspire confidence in team members and encourage them to embrace the change.

6: Provide Support:

Offer support to team members who may be struggling with the change. This could include additional training, resources, or one-on-one coaching.

7: Celebrate Successes:

Celebrate milestones and successes along the way to keep morale high and maintain momentum for the change.

8: Be Patient:

Change can be challenging, and it may take time for team members to fully embrace it. Be patient and supportive throughout the change process.

By communicating change effectively, leaders can help team members understand the need for change, feel engaged in the process, and ultimately support the change. This can lead to a smoother transition and greater success in achieving the desired outcomes.

C: Involving Team Members in the Change Process

Involving team members in the change process is crucial for building buy-in, ownership, and commitment to the change. Here are some strategies for involving team members in the change process:

1: Engage Early and Often:

Start engaging team members early in the change process to gather their input and feedback. Keep them informed and involved throughout the entire process.

2: Solicit Input and Ideas:

Encourage team members to share their ideas, concerns, and suggestions for the change. This can help generate new perspectives and innovative solutions.

3: Empower Team Members:

Empower team members to take ownership of the change by giving them the authority to make decisions and take action within their areas of expertise.

4: Provide Opportunities for Involvement:

Offer opportunities for team members to get involved in planning and implementing the change. This could include serving on change management committees, leading change initiatives, or participating in working groups.

5: Communicate Clearly and Transparently:

Keep team members informed about the progress of the change and the reasons behind decisions. Be open and transparent in your communication to build trust and credibility.

6: Celebrate Successes Together:

Celebrate milestones and successes along the way to keep team morale high and maintain momentum for the change.

7: Provide Support and Resources:

Offer support and resources to help team members navigate the change process. This could include training, coaching, or access to additional information or tools.

8: Listen and Address Concerns:

Listen to team members' concerns and address them in a timely and respectful manner. Show empathy and understanding, and work together to find solutions to any challenges that arise.

By involving team members in the change process, leaders can create a sense of ownership and commitment to the change, leading to a smoother transition and greater success in achieving the desired outcomes.

D: Overcoming Resistance to Change

Resistance to change is a common challenge that leaders face when implementing change in teams. Resistance can stem from various factors, including fear of the unknown, loss of control, and perceived lack of benefit. Here are some strategies for overcoming resistance to change:

1: Listen to Concerns:

Acknowledge and listen to the concerns of team members who are resistant to change. Take the time to understand their perspective and address their concerns.

2: Provide Reassurance:

Provide reassurance to team members that their concerns are being heard and that steps will be taken to address them. Be transparent about the change process and its expected outcomes.

3: Communicate the Benefits:

Clearly communicate the benefits of the change to team members. Help them understand how the change will improve their work environment, processes, or outcomes.

4: Involve Team Members:

Involve team members in the change process by soliciting their input and feedback. Empower them to be part of finding solutions to overcome resistance.

5: Address Misconceptions:

Address any misconceptions or misinformation about the change. Provide accurate and timely information to help dispel myths and rumors.

6: Provide Training and Support:

Offer training and support to help team members adapt to the change. Provide resources and assistance to help them develop the skills needed to succeed in the new environment.

7: Celebrate Small Wins:

Celebrate small wins along the way to keep morale high and show progress towards the desired change.

8: Lead by Example: Demonstrate your commitment to the change by leading by example. Show that you are willing to adapt and embrace the change yourself.

By addressing resistance to change proactively and involving team members in the change process, leaders can help create a more positive and supportive environment for change. This can lead to greater acceptance and success in implementing the desired change.

E: Sustaining Change and Ensuring Long-Term Success

Sustaining change and ensuring long-term success requires ongoing effort and commitment from leaders and team members. Here are some strategies for sustaining change and ensuring long-term success:

1: Monitor Progress:

Continuously monitor the progress of the change initiative. This can help you identify any issues or challenges early on and make adjustments as needed.

2: Celebrate Milestones:

Celebrate milestones and achievements along the way. This can help maintain motivation and momentum for the change initiative.

3: Reinforce the Benefits:

Continuously reinforce the benefits of the change to team members. Help them understand how the change is benefiting them and the organization as a whole.

4: Communicate Openly and Transparently:

Continue to communicate openly and transparently with team members about the progress of the change initiative. Keep them informed about any changes or updates.

5: Address Challenges and Setbacks:

Address any challenges or setbacks that arise during the change initiative. Work with team members to find solutions and overcome obstacles.

6: Lead by Example:

Lead by example and demonstrate your commitment to the change initiative. Show that you are willing to adapt and embrace the change yourself.

7: Provide Support and Resources:

Provide ongoing support and resources to help team members adapt to the change. Offer training, coaching, and other resources as needed.

8: Evaluate and Adjust:

Regularly evaluate the effectiveness of the change initiative and make adjustments as needed. Be willing to adapt your approach based on feedback and results.

By sustaining change and ensuring long-term success, leaders can help the team adapt to new ways of working and achieve their goals. This can lead to improved performance, increased satisfaction, and greater success for the organization as a whole.

Chapter 8: Case Studies in Team Management

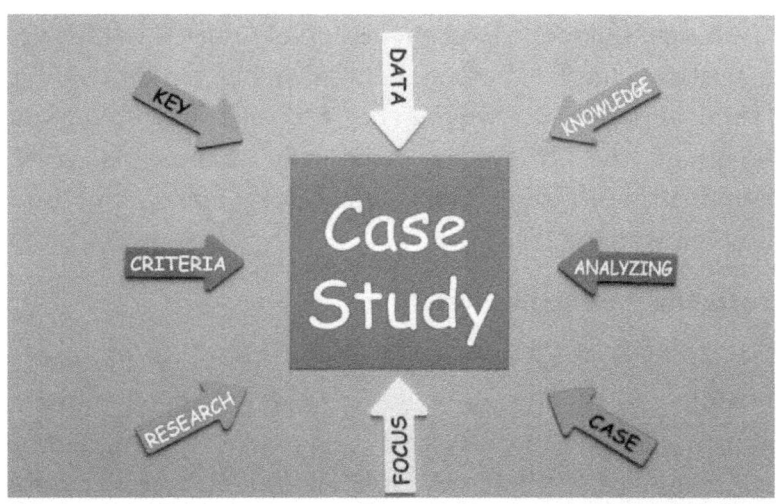

A: Real-Life Examples of Effective Team Management

Real-life examples of effective team management can provide valuable insights into what works in practice. Here are a few examples:

1: Apollo 11 Moon Landing:

The successful moon landing mission of Apollo 11 in 1969 is a classic example of effective team management. NASA's team of scientists, engineers, and astronauts worked together to achieve a seemingly impossible goal, demonstrating exceptional teamwork, innovation, and problem-solving skills.

2: Toyota Production System:

Toyota's production system, also known as "lean manufacturing," is another example of effective team management. The system emphasizes continuous improvement, employee empowerment, and waste reduction, leading to high-quality products and efficient processes.

3: Google's Project Aristotle:

Google's Project Aristotle studied hundreds of teams within the company to identify the factors that contribute to team effectiveness. The project found that psychological safety, dependability, structure and clarity, meaning of work, and impact of work were key factors in effective team management.

4: Amazon's Two-Pizza Team:

Amazon's "two-pizza team" concept is a strategy for keeping teams small and agile. The idea is that teams should be small enough that they can be fed with two pizzas, allowing for easier communication, faster decision-making, and greater accountability.

5: SpaceX's Falcon 9 Rocket Launches:

SpaceX's Falcon 9 rocket launches demonstrate effective team management in the aerospace industry. The company's teams work together to design, build, and launch rockets with remarkable speed and efficiency, revolutionizing space travel in the process.

6: Zappos' Holacracy:

Zappos, an online shoe and clothing retailer, implemented a management system known as Holacracy, which eliminates traditional hierarchical structures in favor of self-managing teams. This approach has led to increased employee engagement and innovation at the company.

These examples illustrate the importance of effective team management in achieving remarkable results. They highlight the value of teamwork, innovation, communication, and leadership in driving success in organizations. Leaders can learn from these examples and apply similar principles in their own teams to achieve similar levels of success.

B: Lessons Learned from Successful Teams

1: Clear Communication:

Successful teams prioritize clear and effective communication. They ensure that team members understand their roles, responsibilities, and goals, and they encourage open dialogue and feedback.

2: Strong Leadership:

Successful teams have strong leaders who provide direction, guidance, and support. These leaders inspire and motivate team members, foster a positive team culture, and lead by example.

3: Collaboration:

Successful teams collaborate effectively, leveraging each team member's strengths and expertise. They value teamwork and cooperation, working together towards common goals.

4: Positive Team Culture:

Successful teams cultivate a positive team culture characterized by trust, respect, and mutual support. They celebrate successes, learn from failures, and create a safe and inclusive environment for all team members.

5: Adaptability:

Successful teams are adaptable and able to respond to changes and challenges quickly. They embrace innovation and are open to new ideas and approaches.

6: Focus on Results:

Successful teams are results-oriented, focusing on achieving their goals and delivering high-quality outcomes. They set clear objectives, track progress, and hold themselves accountable for their performance.

7: Continuous Improvement:

Successful teams are committed to continuous improvement. They regularly assess their performance, identify areas for growth, and implement changes to enhance their effectiveness.

8: Resilience:

Successful teams are resilient and able to bounce back from setbacks. They view challenges as opportunities for learning and growth, and they persevere in the face of adversity.

By learning from successful teams and adopting their practices and strategies, leaders can improve their own team's performance and achieve greater success.

C: Analysis of Challenges Faced and Solutions Implemented

1: Communication Breakdowns:

One common challenge faced by teams is communication breakdowns. This can lead to misunderstandings, delays, and inefficiencies. Successful teams address this challenge by implementing regular communication channels, such as daily check-ins, team meetings, and project management tools. They also encourage open and transparent communication, where team members feel comfortable sharing their thoughts and ideas.

2: Conflicts:

Conflicts within a team can arise due to different perspectives, goals, or personalities. Successful teams address conflicts by promoting a culture of respect and understanding. They encourage team members to resolve conflicts collaboratively, using techniques such as active listening, compromise, and mediation. They also provide training and resources to help team members develop conflict resolution skills.

3: Lack of Motivation:

Maintaining team motivation can be challenging, especially during long projects or when faced with setbacks. Successful teams address this challenge by setting clear goals and milestones, celebrating achievements, and providing regular feedback and recognition. They also encourage teamwork and collaboration, where team members support and motivate each other.

4: Change Management:

Implementing change within a team can be met with resistance and uncertainty. Successful teams address this challenge by involving team members in the change process, communicating openly and transparently about the reasons for the change, and providing support and resources to help team members adapt to the change. They also lead by example, demonstrating their commitment to the change and its benefits.

By analyzing how successful teams have addressed these challenges, leaders can learn valuable lessons on how to manage similar situations in their own teams. They can adopt strategies and best practices that have been proven to be effective, helping to improve team performance and achieve greater success.

Chapter 9: The Future of Team Management

A: Trends in Team Management

1: Remote and Hybrid Work:

The trend towards remote and hybrid work is likely to continue, requiring teams to adapt to new ways of working and communicating. Remote work allows for greater flexibility and can lead to increased productivity, but it also presents challenges such as maintaining team cohesion and communication.

2: Digital Transformation:

The increasing reliance on technology and automation is driving a need for teams to develop new digital skills and capabilities. Teams are leveraging technologies such as artificial intelligence, machine learning, and data analytics to improve efficiency and drive innovation.

3: Diversity and Inclusion:

There is a growing emphasis on diversity and inclusion in the workplace, requiring teams to be more inclusive and culturally aware. Diverse teams are known to be more creative and innovative, but managing diversity effectively requires strong leadership and communication skills.

4: Agile and Flexible Teams:

Agile methodologies and flexible team structures are becoming more common, allowing teams to adapt quickly to changing requirements and priorities. Agile teams are organized around specific projects or goals and work in short, iterative cycles to deliver results quickly and efficiently.

5: Data-Driven Decision-Making:

Teams are increasingly using data and analytics to inform decision-making and improve performance. Data-driven decision-making allows teams to identify trends, forecast future outcomes, and make more informed decisions based on evidence rather than intuition.

Overall, these trends are shaping the way teams are managed and organized, requiring leaders to be adaptable, innovative, and technologically savvy. By embracing these trends, teams can improve their performance, drive innovation, and stay competitive in today's rapidly evolving business landscape.

B: Predictions for the Future of Work

1: Remote Work Will Become More Common:

The trend towards remote work is expected to continue, with more organizations offering remote work options to employees. This shift is driven by advances in technology that make remote work more feasible and by changing attitudes towards work-life balance.

2: Increased Use of AI and Automation:

AI and automation are expected to play a larger role in the workplace, impacting the way teams work and collaborate. While AI and automation can improve efficiency and productivity, they also raise concerns about job displacement and the need for new skills.

3: Focus on Employee Well-being:

There will be a greater emphasis on employee well-being, with organizations implementing policies and programs to support mental and physical health. This includes initiatives such as flexible work hours, mental health resources, and wellness programs.

4: Continued Emphasis on Flexibility:

Flexibility in terms of work hours and location will become more important, as employees seek a better work-life balance. Organizations that offer flexible work arrangements are likely to attract and retain top talent.

5: Greater Emphasis on Skills Development:

With the rapid pace of technological change, there will be a greater emphasis on continuous learning and skills development to keep up with evolving job requirements. Employees will need to adapt to new technologies and acquire new skills to remain competitive in the workforce.

Overall, these predictions suggest a shift towards a more flexible, technology-driven, and employee-centric approach to work. Organizations that embrace these changes are likely to thrive in the future of work.

C: Strategies for Adapting to Changing Work Environments

1: Embrace Digital Tools and Technologies:

Teams should embrace digital tools and technologies to improve communication, collaboration, and productivity. This includes using project management software, communication platforms, and other digital tools to streamline workflows and facilitate remote work.

2: Foster a Culture of Adaptability:

Organizations should foster a culture of adaptability and resilience, encouraging teams to embrace change and learn new skills. This can be done through regular training and development programs, as well as by recognizing and rewarding adaptability in team members.

3: Invest in Training and Development:

Organizations should invest in training and development programs to help teams develop the skills they need to succeed in a rapidly changing environment. This includes both technical skills related to new technologies and soft skills such as communication, collaboration, and adaptability.

4: Prioritize Communication and Collaboration:

Effective communication and collaboration are key to success in a changing work environment, so teams should prioritize these skills. This includes regular team meetings, clear communication channels, and fostering a culture of open and honest communication.

5: Embrace Diversity and Inclusion:

Embracing diversity and inclusion in the workplace can help teams adapt to change more effectively. Diverse teams bring a range of perspectives and ideas to the table, leading to more innovative solutions and better decision-making. Organizations should strive to create an inclusive environment where all team members feel valued and respected.

By embracing these strategies, teams can adapt to changing work environments more effectively and thrive in the face of uncertainty.

Chapter 10: Conclusion

A: Recap of Key Points

Throughout this book, we have explored various aspects of team management, including understanding team dynamics, building a strong team, leadership in team management, managing remote teams, team performance evaluation, developing team skills, leading change in teams, case studies in team management, and the future of team management.

1: Understanding Team Dynamics:

We discussed the importance of team dynamics, the types of teams, stages of team development, and common challenges in team dynamics.

2: Building a Strong Team:

We covered recruiting the right team members, establishing team goals and objectives, creating a positive team culture, effective communication within the team, and encouraging collaboration and creativity.

3: Leadership in Team Management:

We explored qualities of a good team leader, different leadership styles, delegating responsibilities, motivating team members, and handling conflict within the team.

4: Managing Remote Teams:

We discussed the benefits and challenges of remote teams, tools and technologies for remote team management, strategies for effective communication and collaboration, and building trust and accountability in remote teams.

5: Team Performance Evaluation:

We covered setting performance metrics, conducting regular performance reviews, providing constructive feedback, recognizing and rewarding team achievements, and strategies for improving team performance.

6: Developing Team Skills:

We explored training and development programs, building emotional intelligence in team members, encouraging continuous learning and growth, and building resilience in the team.

7: Leading Change in Teams:

We discussed understanding change management, communicating change effectively, involving team members in the change process, overcoming resistance to change, and sustaining change and ensuring long-term success.

8: Case Studies in Team Management:

We presented real-life examples of effective team management, lessons learned from successful teams, and an analysis of challenges faced and solutions implemented.

9: The Future of Team Management:

We discussed trends in team management, predictions for the future of work, and strategies for adapting to changing work environments.

10: Key Points:

Key points covered include the importance of effective communication, collaboration, and leadership in team management, as well as strategies for overcoming challenges and achieving success.

By understanding these key aspects of team management and implementing the strategies discussed, organizations can build strong, high-performing teams that are capable of achieving their goals and adapting to the changing demands of the workplace.

B: Final Thoughts on Effective Team Management

Effective team management is essential for achieving organizational goals and objectives. By understanding team dynamics, building a strong team, and providing effective leadership, managers can create a positive and productive team environment.

1: Understanding Team Dynamics:

It is crucial to understand the dynamics within your team, including the roles and relationships among team members. This understanding helps in fostering a cohesive and collaborative team environment.

2: Building a Strong Team:

Recruiting the right team members, setting clear goals and objectives, creating a positive team culture, and encouraging collaboration and creativity are all key aspects of building a strong team.

3: Providing Effective Leadership:

Good leadership is essential for guiding and motivating team members towards achieving common goals. Effective leaders exhibit qualities such as clear communication, empathy, decisiveness, and problem-solving skills.

4: Managing Remote Teams:

Managing remote teams requires special attention to communication and collaboration. Using tools and technologies to facilitate communication, setting clear expectations, and fostering a sense of trust and accountability are crucial for managing remote teams effectively.

5: Leading Change:

Leading change requires effective communication, involvement of team members in the change process, and overcoming resistance to change. It is important to communicate the reasons for change, the benefits of the change, and to involve team members in finding solutions to overcome resistance.

6: Developing Team Skills:

Continuous learning and development are important for building team skills and capabilities. Providing training opportunities, promoting a culture of learning, and encouraging personal and professional growth are essential for developing team skills.

7: Adapting to Changing Work Environments:

In today's rapidly changing work environment, it is important for teams to adapt to new technologies, ways of working, and market trends. Organizations that are agile and adaptable are more likely to succeed in the long run.

In conclusion, effective team management requires a combination of understanding team dynamics, building a strong team, providing effective leadership, managing remote teams, leading change, developing team skills, and adapting to changing work environments. By focusing on these areas, organizations can build strong, high-performing teams that are capable of achieving their goals and adapting to the changing demands of the workplace.

C: Encouragement for Readers to Implement Strategies Learned

I encourage readers to implement the strategies learned in this book to improve their team management skills and achieve greater success. By applying the principles of effective team management, you can create a positive and productive team environment, overcome challenges, and achieve your goals.

1: Continuous Learning and Adaptation:

Effective team management is an ongoing process that requires continuous learning and adaptation. Stay informed about new trends and best practices in team management, and be open to new ideas and approaches.

2: Creating a Positive Team Environment:

Focus on creating a positive team culture where team members feel valued, motivated, and supported. Encourage open communication, collaboration, and respect among team members.

3: Setting Clear Goals and Expectations:

Clearly define goals, objectives, and expectations for your team. Ensure that team members understand their roles and responsibilities and how they contribute to the overall success of the team.

4: Providing Support and Development Opportunities:

Support the growth and development of your team members by providing training opportunities, coaching, and mentoring. Encourage continuous learning and professional development.

5: Effective Communication:

Communication is key to effective team management. Ensure that communication channels are open and that team members feel comfortable expressing their ideas, concerns, and feedback.

6: Leading by Example:

As a team manager, lead by example. Demonstrate the qualities and behaviors you expect from your team members, such as accountability, integrity, and professionalism.

7: Celebrating Successes:

Recognize and celebrate the achievements and successes of your team. This can help boost morale and motivation, and reinforce positive behavior.

8: Adapting to Change:

Be flexible and adaptable in your approach to team management. Be willing to change strategies and tactics when necessary to meet changing circumstances and challenges.

In conclusion, by implementing the strategies learned in this book, you can become a more effective team manager and lead your team to greater success. Remember, effective team management is not a one-time task, but an ongoing process that requires continuous effort and improvement.

www.ingramcontent.com/pod-product-compliance
Lightning Source LLC
Chambersburg PA
CBHW050327230526
45471CB00005B/2387